FROM SPRUCE TO MAGNOLIA

Poems, Thoughts, and Tales of Nature: Earth, Human, Divine

Belle Schiff

authorHOUSE™

1663 LIBERTY DRIVE, SUITE 200
BLOOMINGTON, INDIANA 47403
(800) 839-8640
WWW.AUTHORHOUSE.COM

First published by AuthorHouse 10/15/04

ISBN: 1-4184-2070-0 (e)
ISBN: 1-4184-2072-7 (sc)

Printed in the United States of America
Bloomington, Indiana

This book is printed on acid-free paper.

Cover art, acrylic on mylar: Carolyn Houg
Back cover photo: Katharine

Inside Artists: Patricia Zimmer, pen and ink
Rintje Raap, photographs
Coral Poser, pen and ink
Kate Wedemire, photographs
Clare, sketches
Andrei Fedorov, photographs
Marjorie Davis, Fawn Rescue, photographs

Technical help: Byron Biller, Robert Fraser, Keith Bergum, Melvin Klassen

For YOU

"Thank you to all those who have accompanied me gently on the road of life."

TABLE OF CONTENTS

SCRIPTURE

2 Chronicles 16.9
For the eyes of the Lord range throughout the earth
To strengthen those
Whose hearts
Are fully committed to him.

Psalm 81:12
So I gave them over to their stubborn hearts.

Christian L. Scheidt, 1708-61
By grace! On this I'll rest when dying
In Jesus' promise I rejoice:
For though I know my heart's condition,
I also know my Savior's voice.
My heart is glad, all grief has flown
Since I am saved by grace alone.

Psalm 117
Praise the Lord, all you nations
extol him, all you peoples:
For great is his love toward us,
And the faithfulness of the Lord
Endures forever.
Praise the Lord.

PREFACE

My earth journey began in Winnipeg, where I was conceived, and continued with my snowstorm birth in a farmhouse cum parsonage some distance from the tiny hamlet of New Sarepta, Alberta which is found in Alberta's parkland region. I was the second of ten children born to my parents. Our mother, an ex-schoolteacher during our childhoods, had her schooling in the city of Winnipeg. She knew the rules of nutrition. Besides that, every one of her children when in primary school proudly brought home "Canada's Food Rules" which our mother laughingly accepted. Without fail she provided us with three delicious and varied meals a day. In fact she raised the vegetables and for many years milked our cow. She supervised our chores.

Our father had been educated in Holland and Germany; he served as a first-aid driver in the front lines in the First World War. A protected younger child on a well-managed estate, he volunteered to serve as a pastor to Lutheran congregations in Western Canada where he adapted cheerfully to his share of outdoor chores. He arrived in Winnipeg in 1926 where he and our mother met.

Julius and Mary consummated their marriage on the 28th day of December, on the Christian "Festival of the Innocents" as my father sometimes jocularly reminded us. Yes, they had been celibate till the night of their marriage.

On a sterner note, the Festival of the Innocents recognizes the death of all two-year olds in Bethlehem at the hands of Herod who wanted to eliminate young Jesus, born under a significant star and destined to die

33 years later under a placard, which jeeringly referred to him as "The King of the Jews".

On my twelfth day of life, due to several factors, my two-year-old elder brother ingested too many chocolate-covered laxative pills, which were an unsolicited and forgotten acquisition during the family move to the country. Finding the package in a bureau drawer among costume jewelry, he swallowed the "candy" and, sadly, his life came to an end. He was buried in the frozen ground of the little church graveyard. On the stone cross headstone are the words from Psalm 63:3 in German which translate as "For your goodness is better than life; my lips glorify you."

"A sister, years later"

In the course of my life I have lived in four Canadian provinces and two American states. I have had the privilege to travel to Germany, Holland, Switzerland (briefly), to Jordan and Israel, and lastly to Mozambique in 1999.

As you will note, my writing has been sparse. I did not keep a journal though at times I wrote a little essay to myself to help clarify my emotional thoughts and lighten my concerns. True to my father's example, in my letters home, I buried my problems and fears, instead expressing daring do in the adventure of life.

Later, in my more mature years, I wrote letters copiously to some trusted friends. They were my journal spread like autumn leaves in the wind. I am going to present my poems chronologically and add two very short stories that deal with grief and hope. I know you will enjoy the work of Vancouver Island artists that illustrate the poems.

I wrote when inspiration, distilled in the crucible of pain or joy, or activated by simple wit, brought words and phrases to my mind. I did not label myself a poet or a writer being embarrassed by the less than classical nature of what I had written. But I now offer my thoughts to those who may find them of interest.

FAMILY PHOTO — Our mother with the lace on her collar is leaning against her father's knee.

The Trickster
Accepting the paradox
Patricia Zimmer

During our rural school years in the Alberta parkland area, coyotes gathered in a row in the field across the road and howled to the moon – or to us? "Paradox" is a word one may hear when Lutheran pastors discuss some of the mysteries of theology.

FOREST COMMUNITY   Artist: Coral Poser

My first encounter with the rainforest in B.C., the westernmost province of Canada bordering on the Pacific Ocean, occurred when I was 17 and traveling east on the continental Canadian National train. B.C. farmers paid the fare for easterners and "prairie chickens" to travel to the Fraser Valley in British Columbia where they would put in long, sunny days harvesting strawberries and raspberries.

Photographer: Kate Wedemire

My friend, Grace Rannankari, has graciously stood in for my blonde sister Elisabeth who is living three provinces to the east.

12

CHILDHOOD POEMS

When people make promises, they always say,

"Tomorrow, Sugar plums",

But "tomorrow" never, never comes.

An uncle, who saw my sister and me standing soberly watching a number of laughing cousins waving colorful balloons as they left eastward in their father's car from the reunion at our grandparents' home in Winnipeg, promised that when we left the next day, we would have balloons too.

The next day, my sister and I sat well mannered with our mother in the railway car headed west WITHOUT balloons.

The disappointment lingered on but was largely dissipated by the writing of the poem some time later. I shared it with my mother in our linoleum-floored kitchen. Mother thought uncle was still an acceptable person.

1936

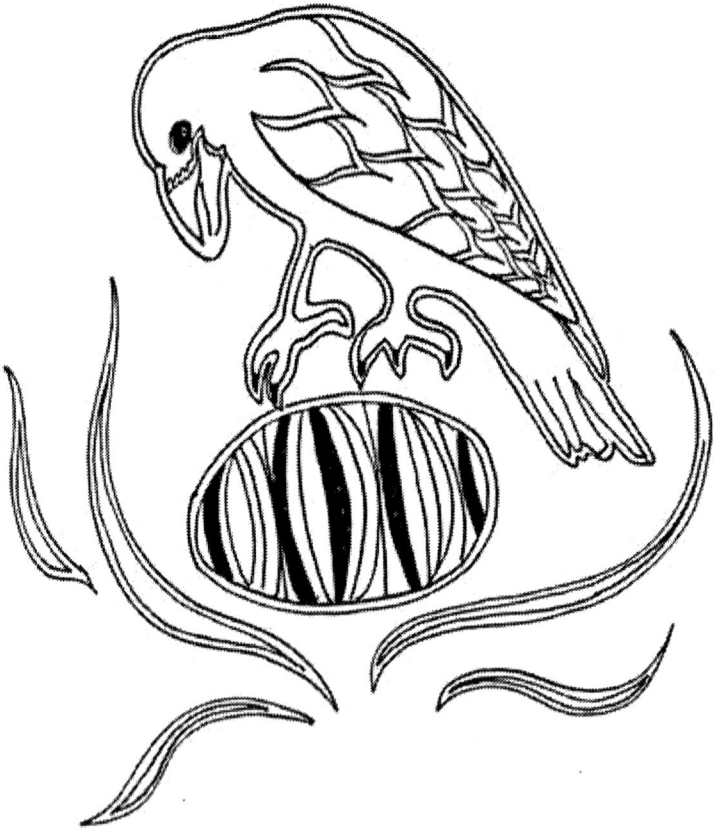

Artist: Patricia Zimmer

The Crow

Crows in western Canada have been interesting and reassuring companions. Once when I walked to school alone, a crow accompanied me, flying from fence post to fence post each time emitting a strong "CAW" which I answered with my own "CAW".

Big shiny, black crow,
I should really like to know
Why you tip up your tail, and bob your head so,
When you go
CAW, CAW, CAW

You steal the birds' eggs,
Then soar into the skies
With those cries,
CAW, CAW, CAW

1939

Belle Schiff

THE ONLY LIMERICK

Artist: Clare

25

The only limerick I can remember:

There was once a young child on a river,

Who said, "This is not very clever:

With the water on top,

If you take a flop,

You might stay down there forever!

WHEN I AM SAFE AND COZY

Artist: Kate Wedemire

WHEN I AM SAFE AND COZY

When I am safe and cozy in my bed
And winds are raging without,
I think the roar must be pirates by Ben Ali led,
Or dragons,
Or redskins with war cries a-shout
Shivery, awful thoughts.

These scary thoughts make me crawl 'neath the flowered quilts,
Where I see woods and lakes and flowers
And birds in the trees with nests abuilt
Who sing to the pattering of fragrant showers.
Beautiful, fairy-like thoughts.

1940

Belle Schiff

QUEEN AND ROLF AND I

Artist: Kate Wedemire

QUEEN AND ROLF AND I

1942

We plough the furrow, Queen and I,
We plough it when the sun is high,
We plough it when the day begins,
And when the sparrow vespers sings.

The seagulls follow in our wake;
They utter strident, wild, sea cries,
They look like foam upon the waves
That from the fertile, brown earth rise.

We eat our well-earned lunch at noon.
While Rolf goes chasing a raccoon,
I lie upon my back and dream
Of splashing in a cold, blue stream.

1980

And now I say to Rolf, "How sweet,
If folks in all the world could eat
Of food from their own home and clime,
Keeping their hearts at healthy prime.

1986

So sang the plough-boy of my youth,
A knowing citizen of strength and couth.*
Long may his kind know joy in living
Long may the earth have food for giving.

World-wide hunger in the global village
Needs my green, organic tillage
Great earth citizens we all will be
When we learn to live sustainably.

*couth: good-natured, friendly, well-bred

In 1942, riding in the family "V8", traveling westward, I glanced to the green fields at right and was impressed by a boy about my own age independently plowing the tree-edged field with his plough-horse. Rolf is the boy's canine companion. Queen is the working horse.

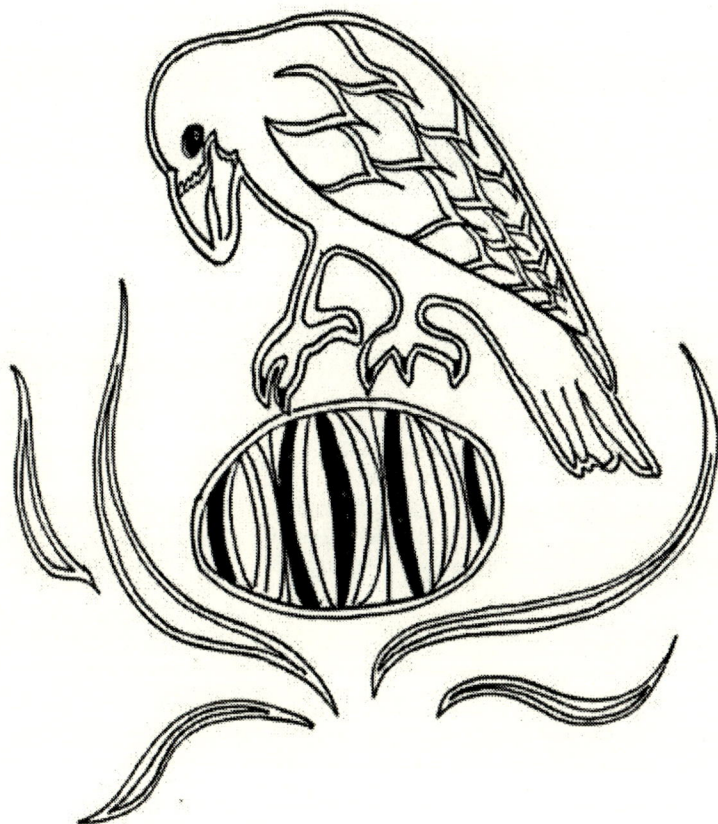

Artist: Patricia Zimmer

LATER POEMS

THE TREE LEAVES

The tree leaves are rustling deep into the night.
They whisper, they murmur while it is night.
They sing songs their ancestors sang long ago
Of things that are hidden and no man may know.
They whisper of mysteries never been solved;
They murmur of secrets never been told.

Dark clouds in the sky
And waves coming high;
But the tree leaves still whisper and murmur and sigh.

Written about midnight, 1944 in the sleeping porch of
a lakefront cabin on Sylvan Lake, Alberta.

FRESHMAN YEAR

Photo: Kate Wedemire

FRESHMAN YEAR

There are men that we abhor,
Who, like Tracy's sophomore,
Women's morals do deplore

Rigoletto's duke we hate
And that royal Henry VIII –
And that scoundrel, Don Giovanni
Who of morals hadn't any.

They worry about motes, it seems,
Despite the size of private beams.
We won't listen to their pratings,
Till they bolster their own ratings.

1950

I attended Dr. Tracy's freshman English course. In some context he remarked that sophomore men tend to be cynical about women. As the class went on, I, in high dudgeon, tossed off the above lines. At intermission, some male classmates were very impressed and urged me to put the poem on the professor's desk. I did not do so, not knowing which way the wind would blow. Dr. Tracy was an Englishman with clipped, correct speech. His classes were excellent.

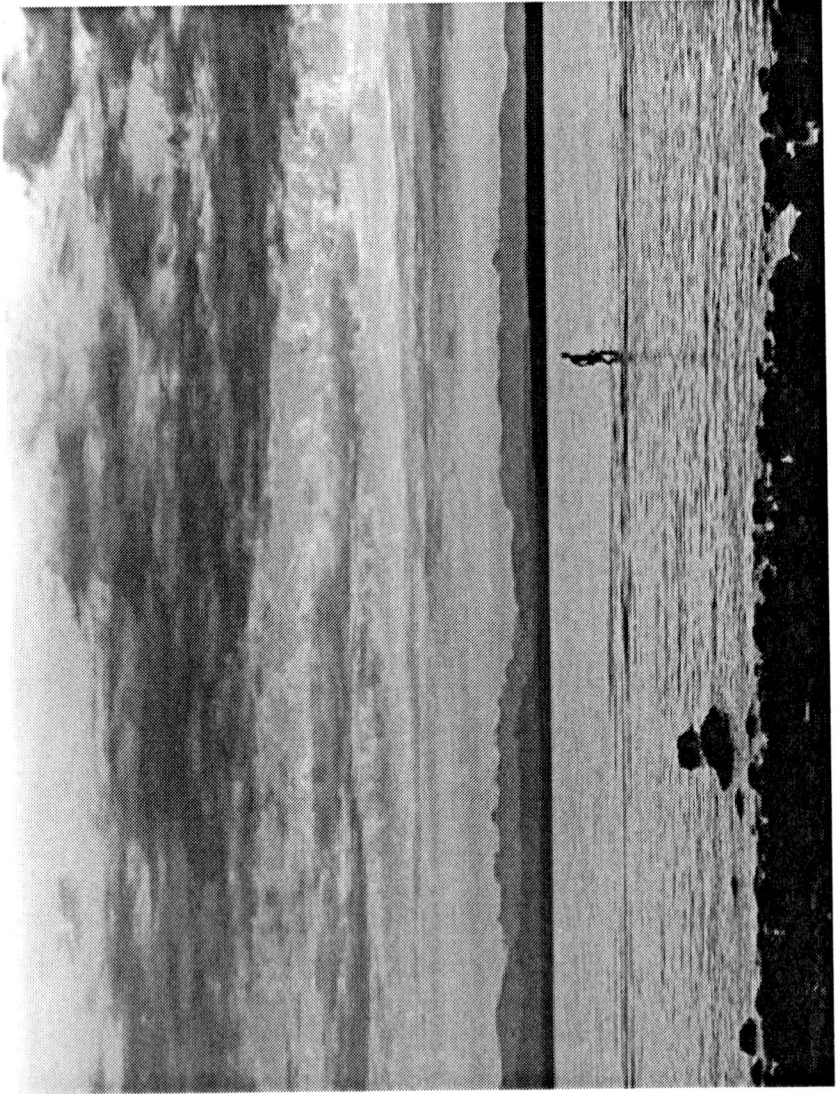

SKY, CLOUDS, MOUNTAINS AND SEA

Photographer: Riintje Raap

Photograph by Rintje Raap of a view from Cortes Island
looking toward Miracle Beach.

SKY, CLOUDS, MOUNTAINS AND SEA

The cool, the distant, the blue
The long long line lying low.
Measureless blue
billowing layers of white
Blue, shadowing angles.
Evanescent, twinkling,
deeply moving, eternal sea.

Change and eternity living together,
Time and timelessness
form and formlessness
Remote, silvery, uncomprehended.

Evolving past, hovering future,
probing and vanishing present.
Meaning and beauty,
Timelessness.

Experienced and written in early 1960s. Shortly after
we had enjoyed this view looking outward from Miracle
Beach on Vancouver Island, heavy rain began to fall.
We cooked a cozy supper in the door of our tent.

KLAPPERN UND KNISTERN

Artist: Patricia Zimmer

Klappern und knistern in der Küche

Schlägt eine Trommel

Oder

Summt eine Mücke?

(Original)

Clatter and clangor in the kitchen

Is it the sound of a drum

Or

A mosquito's hum?

(Translation)

1966

After a heavy siege, I retreated home, sleeping and drowsing till mid-morning. The outside workers having left, the one who worked from home was clearing the kitchen. In a surreal mood, I was unsure whether the times (and the Almighty) were calling for immediate action or whether I could let myself be lulled by the ordinary sounds of a peaceful summer's day.

WHO CARES FOR THE WEATHER

Artist: Patricia Zimmer

WHO CARES FOR THE WEATHER: I DO!

Some say when it rains that it gives them chilblains
Some say when it snows that it freezes their toes.
Some say when it's cloudy it makes them more rowdy.

Why not read the weather
as though it were clever?
love the sun
love the rain
love the snow
love the blow, blow, blow, blow, blow!

O weather is honest, and weather is true. It's coming from God and it's talking to you.

So look for the pleasure in all kinds of weather – take it easy, go with it
be smart as a robin
a frog
or an elk .

Adjust in your own way:

Talk back to the sun and sing with the clouds.
Try ducking
Try jumping
Try being blasé.

Who cares for the weather: I do!

1972

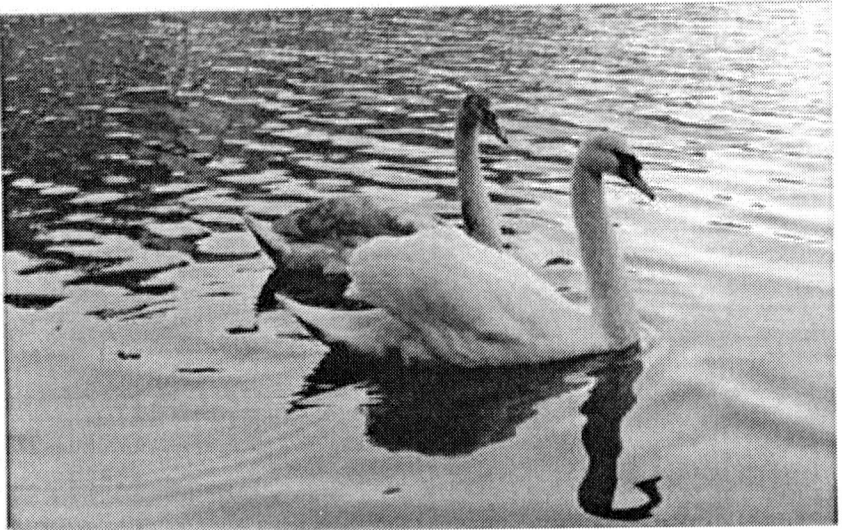

YOUR PHYSICAL PERFECTION

Artist: Riintje Raap

Your physical perfection

In all its precision,

Leads me to distraction.

Oh what shall I do

With my Teutonic lumps

And my ton-nish passions?

Circa 1970

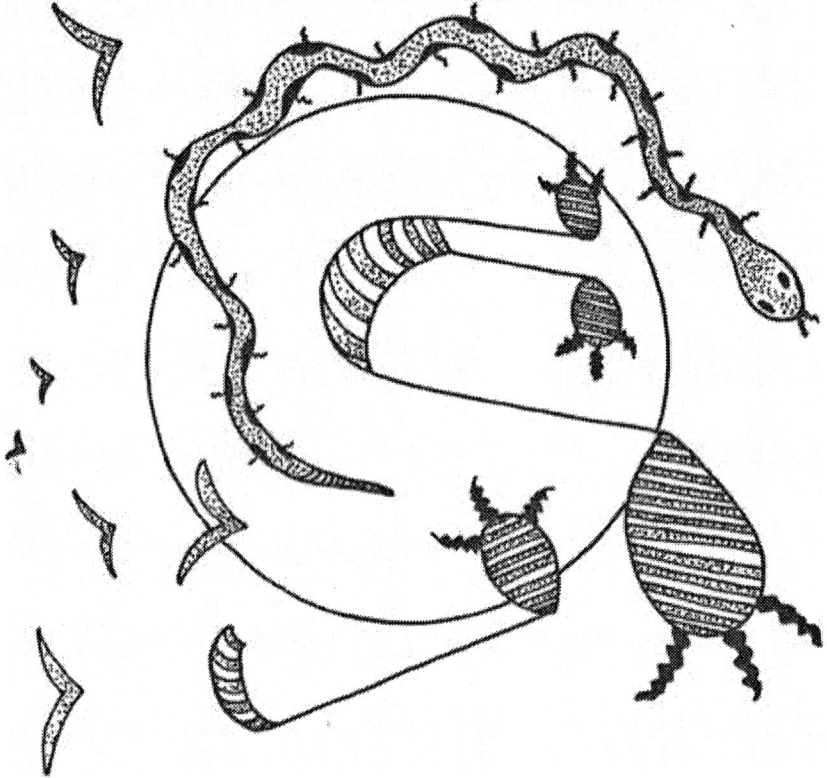

ODE TO AN UNBROKEN DAY

Artist: Patricia Zimmer

January, 1977

This apartment building was spread out like a two-story motel. Across the road were the playing fields of Victoria High School. This was where the feathered creatures noisily greeted the morning, then flew on.

ODE TO AN UNBROKEN DAY

At half past eight, having accepted
A night with little sleep,
I rise.

The nocturnal hours were neither dreamed
Nor deep.
Again the occupant a few suites over
And one up
Thanked his guests in voice too loud, too free
To allow rest.

The waking dream was filled with snakes
Like lizards
Noisily and fiercely winging through
The grass sharply angled.

Nature has since spoken in the form
Of ducks or gulls
Whose cries and clangor filled
The air above the grass next door
Full over an hour ago.

By Arcadian time, it seemed
I should arise, wed to the sounds
That rent the skies.

Now, it is wise to rise
Before the more pedestrian crawl
Of human lives
Slows down my blood
And makes my flesh go thud,
And fall, backwards in time,
From that first winging through the skies.

A DAY OF PAIN

Artist: Carver unknown. Purchased in a shop in Jerusalem in 1998.

Photo: Andrei Fedorov

A DAY OF PAIN

"Thus the heavens and the earth were finished, and
all the host of them. And on the seventh day God had
finished his work which he had done and he rested on
the seventh day from all his work which he had done in
creation."

God's work thus far had not
been overdone, for
At the end of every day, he said,
"That's good."

But soon thereafter creature
work begun, a day of pain.

For man and beast both
make mistakes
of heart
of brain
of will.

How much pain does the earth's
story hold?

Is grief too deep to find a home
In human breast?

Is pain intelligent and known
How often?

So man-wo-man can stand and
be alone
And know our full creation,
Accepting the full measure
And extent of pain, which is, for us

the simple truth among
our different states of being.

What is the full measure of our pain
This side of dissolution?

A day for weeping, or
a day for dry-eyed,
continuing existence,
from whence at last again,
we sleep, we eat,
we celebrate along with tree top winged bird,
its gentle ecstasy.

We carry on.

1977

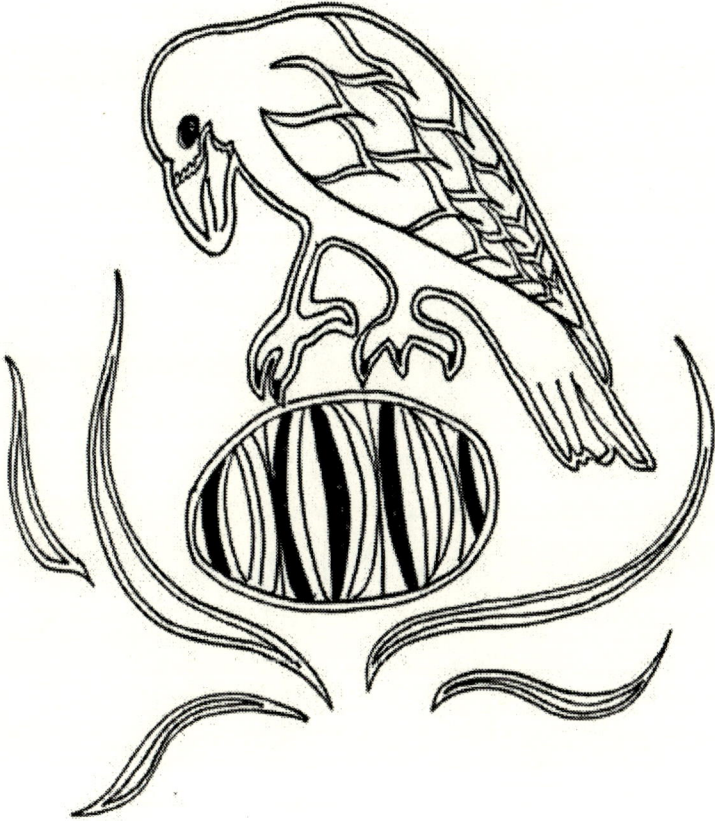

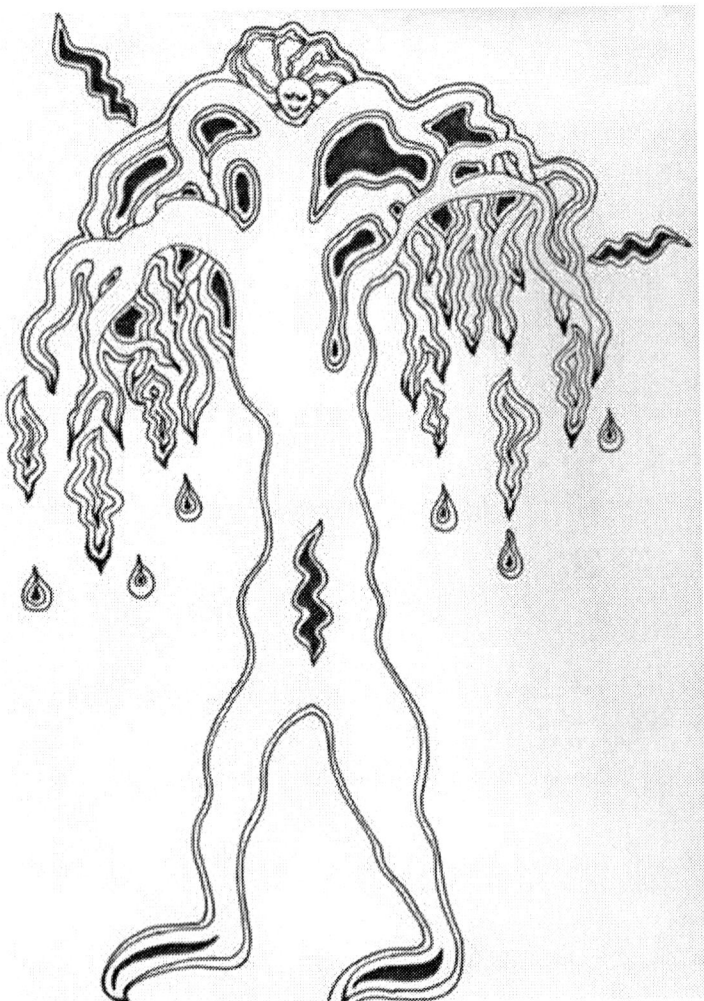

BENDING LOVE, BENDING ANGER

Artist: Patricia Zimmer

BENDING LOVE, BENDING ANGER

"And Jesus entered the temple of God and drove out all who sold and bought in the temple, and he overturned the tables of the moneychangers and the seats of those who sold pigeons. He said to them, "It is written, 'My house shall be called a house of prayer, but you make it a den of robbers.'"

When anger has a clear track
through the emotions,

When anger has a clear track
through a mind equipped with
concepts and with sentences of words,

When anger talks through muscles
on a centered body,
it leaves its inner source and illumes.

When anger rides on others
when anger harms the stranger to the cause, when anger is misplaced and bent, when anger has no words

what shall we do?

1977

MAN, OFF-CENTRE

Snapshots by author

MAN, OFF-CENTRE

Man, off-centre
wishes to shuffle through life
avoiding pain
merchandising and messing.
Inventing painkillers, looking the other way,
taking advantage.

When does pain begin – how
is it met?
Should it be fully recognized
before assuaged?

Should effect seek cause?

How many roar in anger?
Who stares in disbelief?

The height of fury is a good defense
when pain is wrought by human
agency, for its offensive
routs the inciter of the wound.

Who stays to hit again?

and who absorbs the grief
when man-wo-man,
knocked from the centre of their being
no longer feel
with centred selves
the onslaught of the dislocation
which brings them pain?

Is pain a beauty?
Are mothers cowards
Who seek to assuage?

Does the individual
dry-eyed or screaming,
find her own way through?

1977

T'SOU-KE, THEN AND NOW --- Aboriginal Face

Artists: Darlene George & Gord Langston

T'SOU-KE, THEN AND NOW --- The Princess Royal

Artist: Tony Gsellman

T'SOU-KE, THEN AND NOW --- Bronze Bust of Manuel
Quimper donated by King of Spain

T'SOU-KE, THEN AND NOW --- Dressed clay figures

Artist: Dorita Grant

T'SOU-KE, THEN AND NOW

Manuel Quimper came to our land,
And here he was met by natives so grand.

They fell for each other,
And slept oh so sweet

To the tunes of the breakers,
The sighing of pines ---

The silent song of Eternity
Gave them no grief

For eternity quivers and leaps!

It flows from a humble motif.

Manuel Quimper, born in Lima, Peru and Captain of the sailing ship Princess Royal, approached East Sooke on Vancouver Island in June 1790. The ship's log notes, on June 23, 1790, 'DAY DAWNED WITH THE SKY CLEAR, THE LAND ALL COVERED WITH MIST AND THE WIND CALM...THREE CANOES OF INDIANS CAME OUT FROM THE FORT AND INSISTED WE SHOULD GO IN...AND IT WAS VERY GOOD"

I was moved; this little poem embodies my wish that the peace and joy of eternity will resolve the griefs caused by human variance from the good for those who desire it, wherever they may be.

The Sooke Festival Society was formed as the 200th anniversary approached of the landing June 23, 1790 of the first European vessel in the Strait of Juan de Fuca. Most memorable was the re-enactment of the event on a sunny spring day in June 1990 at a public park on

Belle Schiff

Whiffin Spit in Sooke. Two permanent monuments were unveiled. T'Souke Chief Larry Underwood unveiled a memorial drawn by Darlene George and carved by Gord Langston: an aboriginal portrait within the winds of time. Spanish ambassador Fournier unveiled the carving of the sailing ship Princess Royal by Tony Gsellmann. The bronze bust of Manuel Quimper was donated by the King of Spain the following year.

I enjoyed this day; its memory stays with me.

I AM a fine and slender stalk;

My leaves are soft like lettuce,

A joyous green: each leaf a separate story.

The lower leaves soft segments unevenly edged, melding into casual triangles:

Each higher leaf a long and narrow tongue of green,

Crowned by a scatter of umbels carrying tiny star-like flowers, five-stamened and five-petaled, each brilliant yellow petal a tiny rectangle with perfectly serrated outer edge.

I AM yellow FREEDOM crying high and endlessly into space

In my joy of fulfilled growth from the gifts within the seed,

I AM CONTENT

I SING MY SONG

I HOLD MY PLACE.

This was the autumn message I received from the last blossoming stalk of a Vancouver Island native plant found in a clearing among wooded hills.

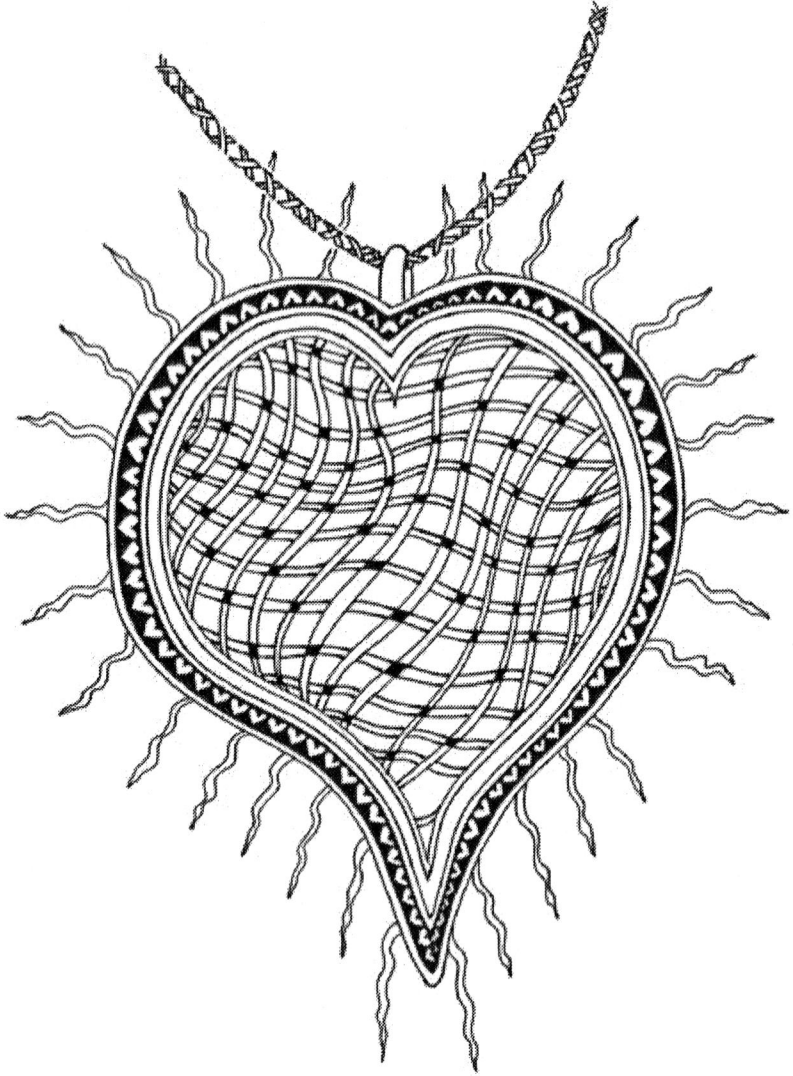

A POEM FOR MOUSIE AND BABY

Artist: Patricia Zimmer

A POEM FOR MOUSIE AND BABY

You, who have endured on native soil,
In the land of the wild rose, the pussy willow,
And the tiny bluebell.

Hear me, a wanderer from place to place.

Ah, what sport was made of me
As I struggled to endure.

What the Lord
had in store
was not clear.

Deep within were strivings strong,

All around were eyes of pain.

Should one understand the world? Oneself? The way
of the Lord?

All three were tasks that brought on tension and
dissension,

Such truths I hardly need to mention to
Persons who have walked the length.

Of inner grief you've had your own.

But now, at last, you sit at home and listen
To your husbands groan and mutter

And still, you cause their hearts to flutter.

Belle Schiff

In 1994, I wrote this rather imaginary poem for two Alberta sisters, friends since childhood.

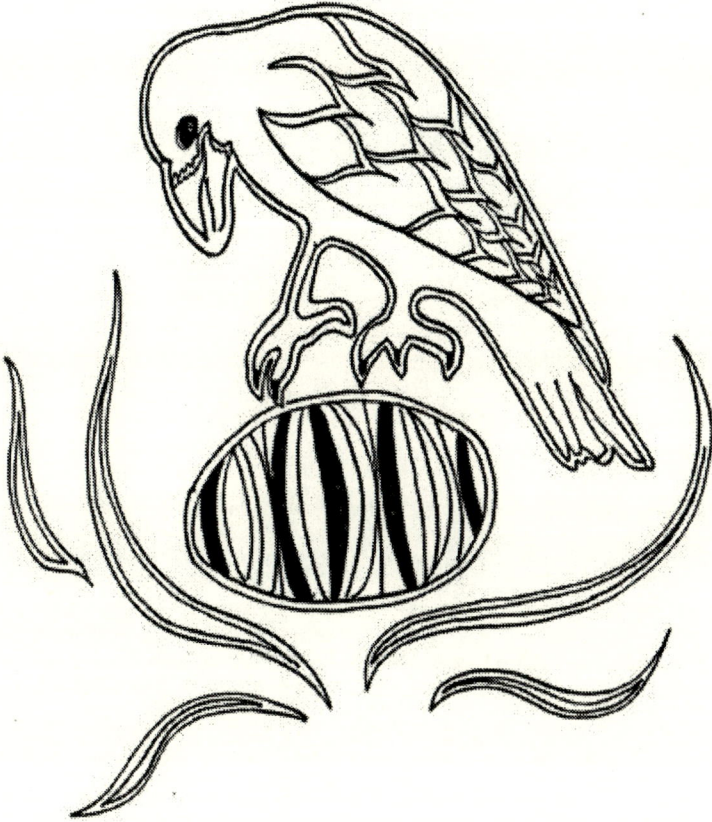

TO A FRIEND

Photographer: Kate Wedemire

TO A FRIEND

Roses bloom in my soul
When the grace of your spirit
Brings order and cleanliness to life.

This was originally inspired when my middle sister and
I shared housekeeping chores. Please give it a broad
and also a spiritual application.

1994

TO YOU, WILMA

Artist: Patricia Zimmer

TO YOU, WILMA

On my 64th birthday, I cast off the burden and wrote the following message to a new "me".

"To you Wilma
a Special Person –
like a snowflake –
which is true to its own being,
which has its own lifespan,
and which melts gracefully
into Eternity
May eternal peace be yours
A gift of faith.

I wanted to bring you a gift of Peace this day
This day of a lunar month in earth-time when you
entered this world from the womb of your mother,
from your nine-month home in the womb of a
woman.

A day of the human year which you share with untold numbers of humans, both living and onward.

Peace

        Love

                Bliss

January, 1994

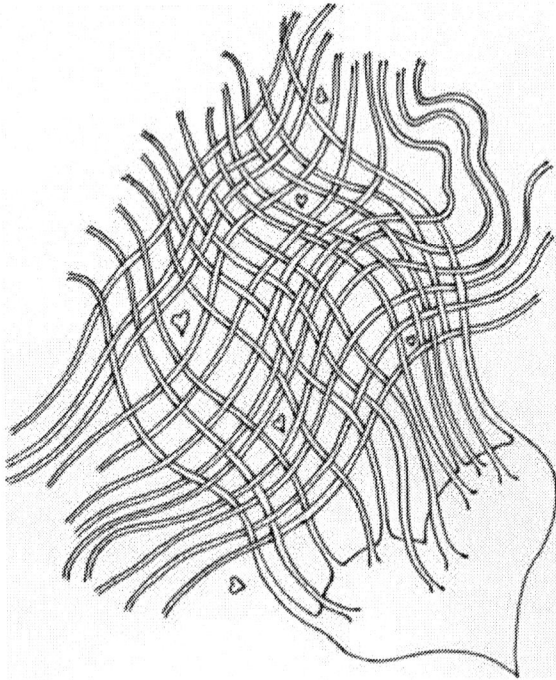

THE WEAVING OF THE HEART

Artist: Patricia Zimmer

THE WEAVING OF THE HEART: A HEALING RESOLUTION

Where mind lacks knowledge, breadth and depth,
The heart can work, regardless

For the heart, when attuned to divine wisdom,
Can turn the threads to spiritual might

Making of all a lesson, and a turning
Within the warmth and heat of the divine Will

The will that all should be saved and come to
the knowledge of heart's love, and of dependence
on the divine order within which true life is supported,
engendered.

Where the gift of atonement can heal, correct, lead
To repentance, bliss of forgiveness, and health.

Morning of May 26, 1994

Psalm 16: 7: I will praise the Lord, who counsels,
Even at night my heart instructs me.

Belle Schiff

After looking up a word in the dictionary one day in 1995, my mind became agile and playful as I flipped the pages and caught some delicious words out of which, The Dictionary Trio, poems 1, 2, and 3 sprang to life.

THE DICTIONARY TRIO

1.   Ode to Sanity and Sound Judgment

As the river flows so gently
Through the hills of Sooke
I think of you
My friend   my guardian

My imposter!

The arrow flies upward
Into your heart.

Will it bring death
Or consubstantiality?

COMPASSION FLOWS LIKE THE RAIN

UPON US ALL.

Our hearts are transformed,

Reformation is begun.

For one week
We are silent

THEN

As rivers flow, and food plants grow,

OLD ADAM ARISES
ANCIENT EVE TREMBLES

We are at it again!

1995

ODE TO A SANTON

Photographer: Kate Wedemire

2.   Ode to a Santon
(Moslem monk or hermit)

Sir Santon, we beg you

please come to our land,

for we hear that a Moslem

greatly reveres

the One

who gave him to the Earth

his/her   M O T H E R

and all other

MOTHER   PERSONS

              persons

              persons

1995

SANITY, MON SANS-CULOTTE

Photographer: Kate Wedemire

You smell so sweetly of sansevieria.

Or would you rather taste of oyster

As we dance the salterello?

Or would you rather smell of seaweed

As I drag you from the river
To the cottage

where the

porridge and the German salad greet
you?

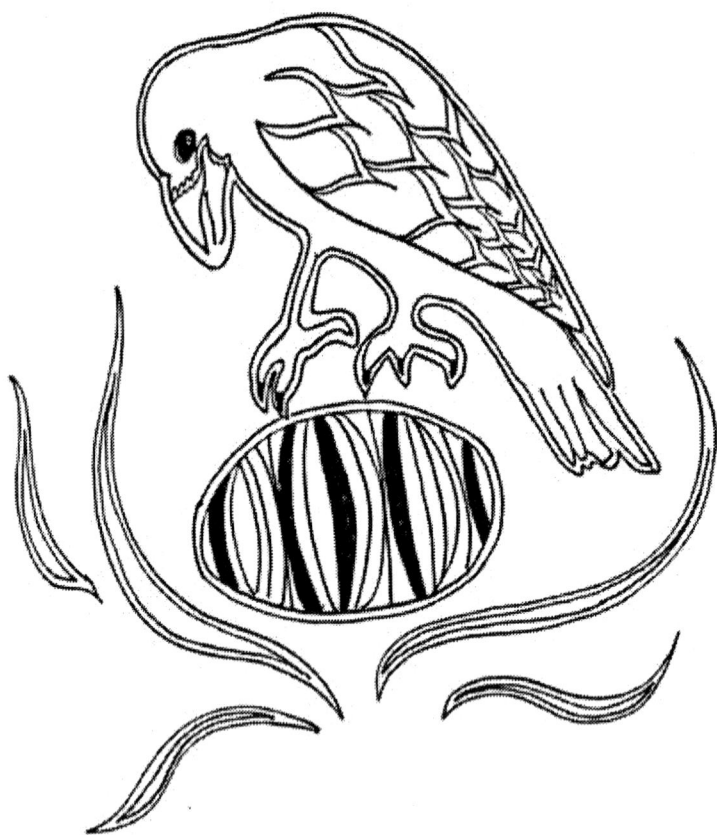

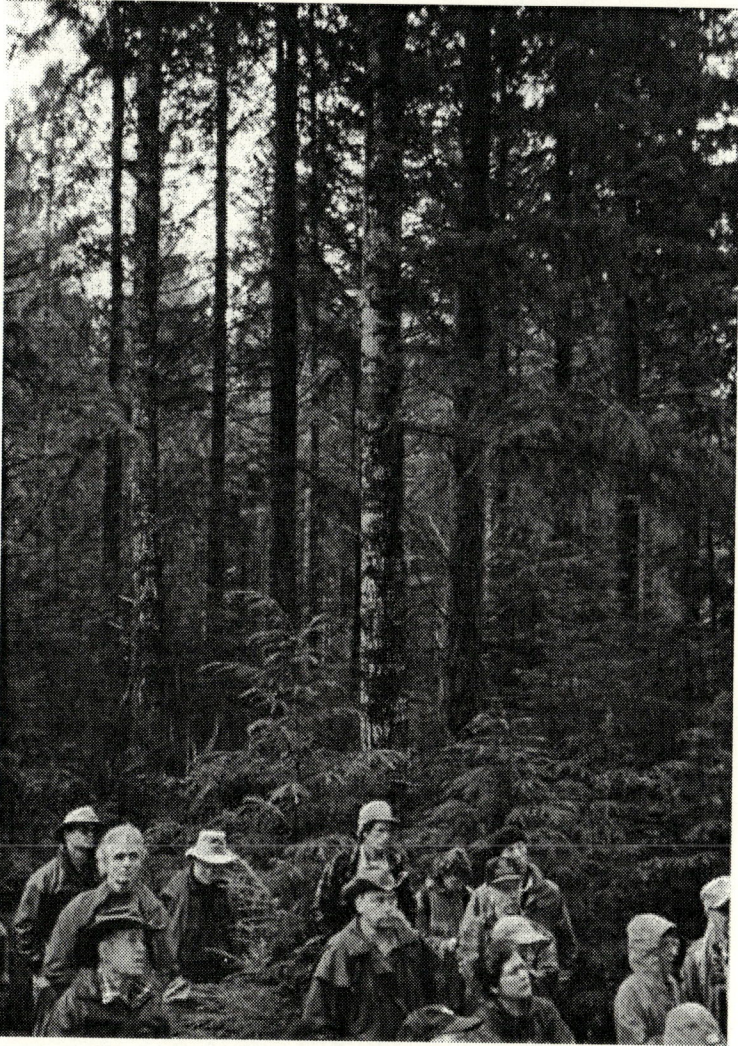

THE SOUL, CHRISTWOOD NEAR JORDAN

Photo: courtesy Sierra Club archives

Newborn

One month old

THE SOUL, CHRISTWOOD NEAR JORDAN
Photos: Marjorie Davis, Director, Fawn Rescue
Organization, Kenwood, California

THE SOUL, CHRISTWOOD NEAR JORDAN

Forty-seven humans on a bus named SMILE
An holistic crucible near the Pacific with all its rivers.

A slight fawn near Christwood.

A slight fawn pauses, having crossed the road a moment before our bus – named SMILE – as we journey home towards the city, leaving behind us these forested hills in various stages of growth and regrowth:

The fawn seems to comprehend that we searching humans love/need nature's token of LIFE that moves by CHOICE, not only by fear or need or greed.

This tiny fawn, glancing back from her paused and fragile presence, says quietly to all 47 of us,

"Here I am."

1995

Thursday, August 24, 1995: Date of an 8:30 a.m. to 3:00 p.m. bus journey with nature walks and information, hosted by Western Forest Products, to their Jordan River, south Vancouver Island logging site. Our bus was moving slowly, yet the tiny fawn's risky yet composed arrival at the left side of the road seemed like an act of God. The fawn seen on that August day may have been two weeks old.

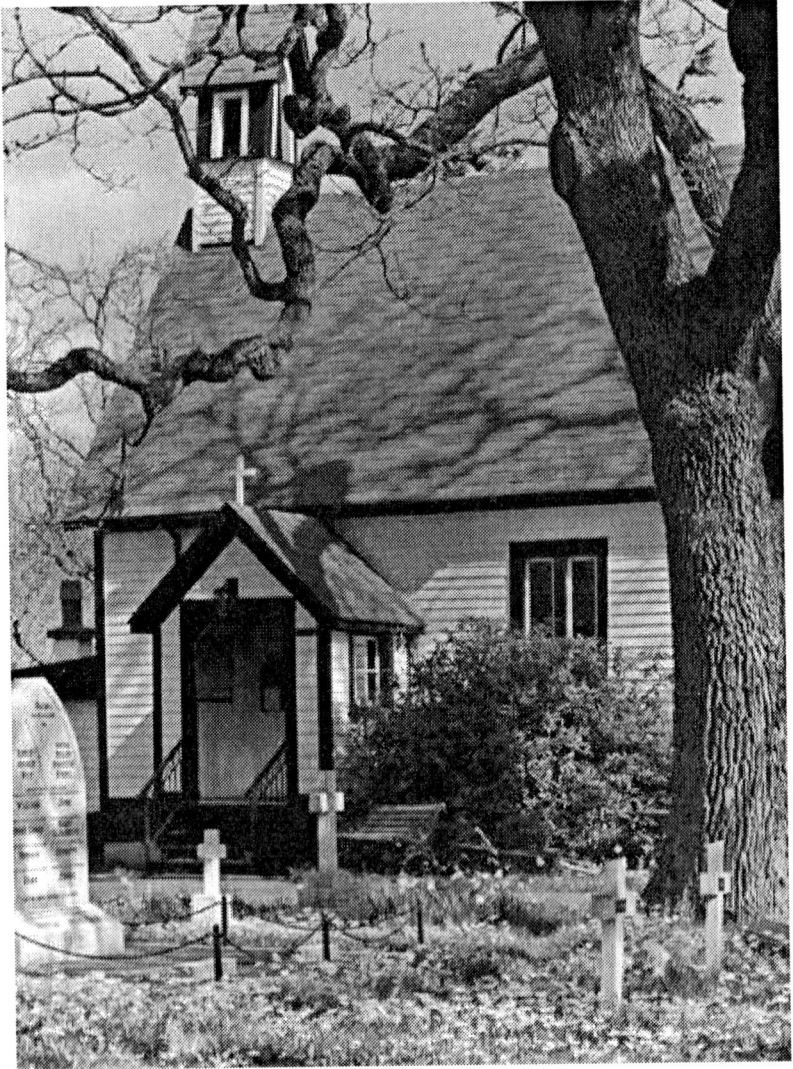

CONVERSATIONS FROM DREAMLAND

Photographer: Andrei Fedorov

A short play

CONVERSATIONS FROM DREAMLAND

Setting: a quiet country cemetery near Victoria, B.C. On stage, a deciduous tree, simple gravestones, and a rustic bench; if possible a wooden fence. Man is not on stage; his pinched voice should seem to come from the branches of the tree.

Persons: the spirit of a man of 33; a woman of 50

MAN to himself, slowly, reflectively: "Here she is again --coming over to my grave. I never knew her. I can tell she is relaxing herself when she comes here. She doesn't come with flowers for anyone, just brings a magazine and sometimes a book to write in. Has she been ill? -- She walks kind of slow and careful. I feel good about her: quiet, thoughtful eyes. Wonder if she'll ever attune to me."

"HELLO, LADY"

Lady sits down on a rustic bench, opens her book, but meditates more than she reads.

MAN: "Heck if I had known a woman like that. We could have talked about a few things. Not that it would have helped. Those rats had it in for me.......When that started up again, I just finished things off........I just finished.........I just"

LADY: "just finished things?
...............................Who are you?"

MAN: "Who am I? I'm me. Dead as a doornail but still talking."

LADY: "Still talking?"

The wind rustles through the grass, a bird sings, insects buzz, ...a fence creaks.

Woman looks around lightly towards the sources of these sounds, and falls into reverie. After some time she startles: the younger man has impinged on her consciousness again.

MAN: calling, "Hello.......Hello........Hello"

LADY: "Hello?"

MAN: "I'm still here. I want some attention."

LADY: "But,.......How could you be here?"

MAN: "Well, I left too soon...............I'm not ready to go on further-----I want to solve the problems I was dealing with---I want to be respected and loved by persons today. I'm crying for you."

THE END

1996

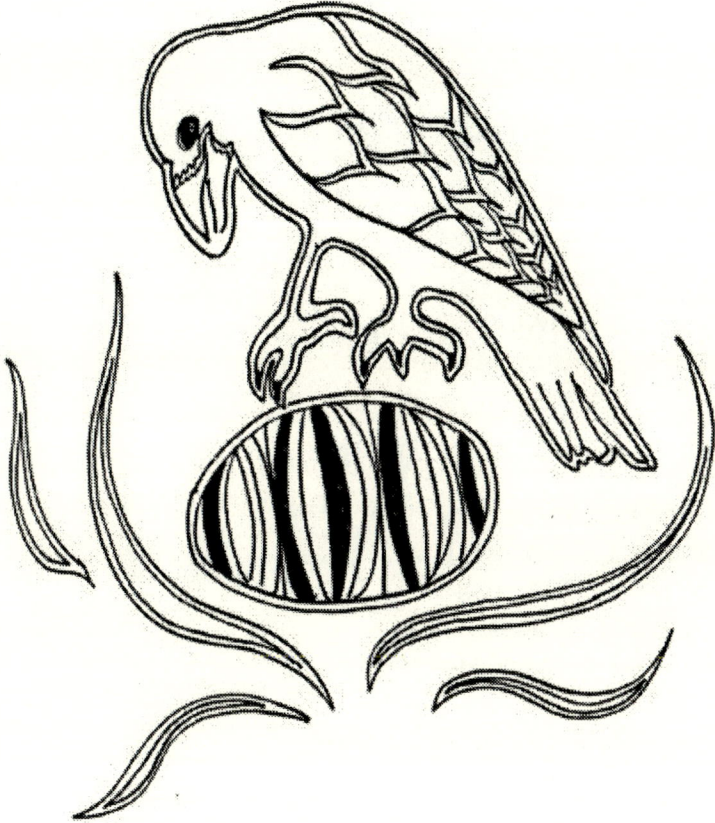

Belle Schiff

TURN THE PAGE

Turn the page
To days gone by
To innocence lost,
When life was new
in the burst of spring.

Turn the page
To the heat of summer
When growth matures
And colors dance brilliantly
in frenzied activity.

Turn the page
to days growing shorter,
When nature's produce
Is abundant
Upon dry falling leaves.

Turn the page
To the frost of winter
Drawing heat from life
Leaving other springs
To future generations.

Erika Binder (by permission)

Recently, as we have entered the 21st century, Erika, my friend since childhood, sent me this poem sharing her septuagenarian viewpoint. I like the poem and I find it a neat summing up.

Seasons of the Year

TURN THE PAGE

TURN THE PAGE

Seasons of Life

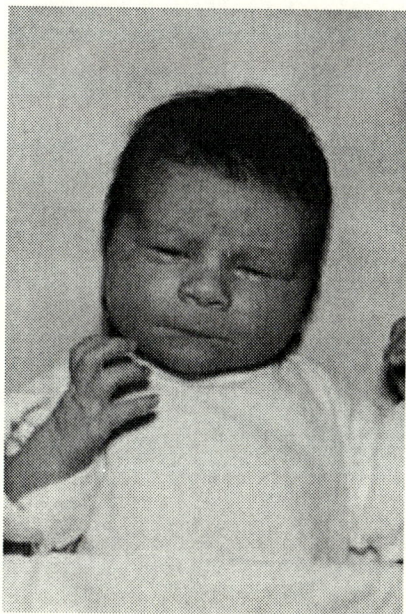

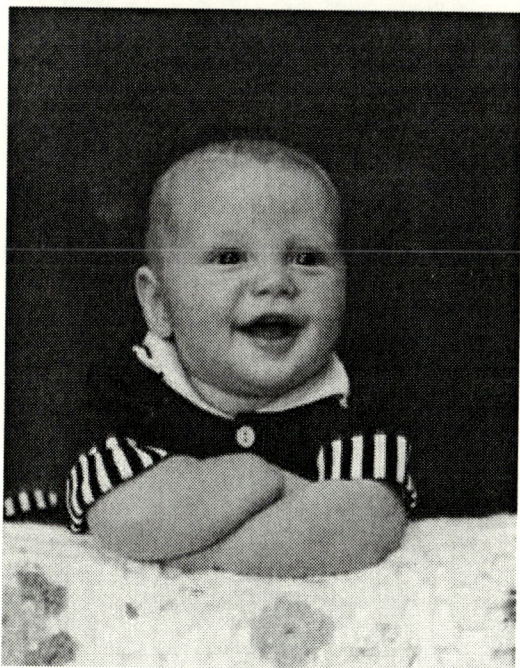

TURN THE PAGE

TURN THE PAGE

TURN THE PAGE

TURN THE PAGE

TURN THE PAGE

TURN THE PAGE

TURN THE PAGE

TURN THE PAGE

TURN THE PAGE

TURN THE PAGE

TURN THE PAGE

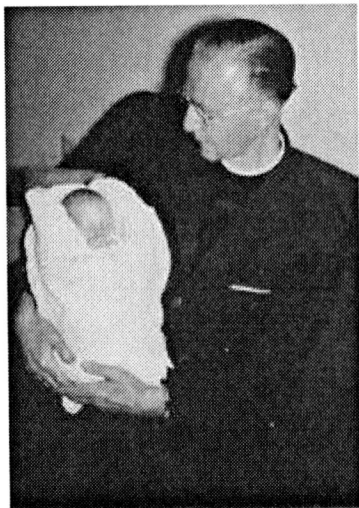

TURN THE PAGE

TURN THE PAGE

V. Two Stories of Intersecting Earth Journeys

SURVIVAL STAMINA AND SPIRITUAL HOPE

One of my friends, Clare, is a single person with three school-age children. She was born in Cambodia of Chinese-origin parents.

Of comely appearance and gentle, if sometimes imperious, and sometimes humorous, personality, she suffers from unshakeable anxieties.

The third youngest in a family of thirteen siblings, she was declared at birth as a bad luck child who was stupid and who would in future sell her body for money. Her mother, an uneducated, country person took this seriously, spurning Clare and repeatedly sending her away. Clare's paternal grandfather had been well to do, knowing eight Chinese dialects and three other languages. He exported lumber to Cambodia. With the economic breakdown caused by war, he lost his fortune. His son, Clare's father, fled to Cambodia where he married the daughter of a prosperous farmer. Gifted in numerous skills, he was able to provide a good life for his family.

When I first met her, Clare was in deep distress. A Buddhist by religion, she repeated often, "I am not lucky. I must have been a very bad person in a past life." Her greatest immediate problems were her unreliable health and the fact that subsidized housing, being in gravely short supply, had not been available to her. Faced with eviction shortly after I first met her, we canvassed subsidized housing units unsuccessfully. She hopefully moved into a small back apartment available in a pleasant district, for a time evading the fact that the rent exceeded her income by one hundred dollars. Since then she has had the fortune to move into a ground floor apartment that is more within her financial reach. However, balancing needs with income still is a daunting challenge.

At eight year of age, Clare was sent to the home of her grandfather's second wife in Viet Nam to receive schooling. At age 12 she was moved to the home of her "grandmother", the first wife, of whom she was afraid. At age 14, she was expected to marry a 40-year-old man. She ran away to her home in Cambodia, but the war there had destroyed the family home and had scattered the family. Clare fended for herself, wandering from village to village in search of her family. She ate out of garbage cans and sold saleable salvage; sometimes she was given food in exchange for cooking and cleaning. She stole food put out for dogs.

One family for whom she cooked and cleaned, hired a teacher to come to their home. As lessons for the children went on, Clare stood outside under the window to listen and learn.

For a while Clare received food for helping in the kitchen and cleaning in a Buddhist temple weekdays. Curious about practices she observed, she asked the monks many questions. A monk and nun took her on kindly for teaching in Buddhist moral principles. If she stole, she should pray and say she was sorry to the Buddha.

Clare did not feel satisfied with the vegetarian diet of the monastery. She craved chicken. She was encouraged to pray to the Buddha and she might get lucky and in future would eat chicken. Clare says she was very funny as a little girl and for this reason she was well liked. "I lied and joked", she says. If money was dropped

95

she quickly put her foot on it, saying in her thoughts, "Sorry God, sorry God, but I really want money."

In her family home, Clare had been sexually abused by a brother and an uncle. In 1984, seeking shelter and sustenance, Clare came to the house of a very controlling woman. Here she became a virtual prisoner after a son of the house blindfolded and gagged her before raping her. Against her will, she became a tormented victim of the sex trade. Today her sleep is still disturbed by visions of the endless men she endured. Once she escaped, only to return later because of severe hunger. Three times she attempted suicide – by pills, by hanging, by drowning – but each time she was discovered and saved.

At age 16, Clare escaped a second time and reached a refugee camp in Thailand where she says she experienced her first kiss. At age 17 her first child was born, and at age 18 she left for Canada with the family of her partner. They were all sponsored by a Christian church in Canada where they received help in adjusting to this new, strange country. They learned about the Christian faith. Unable to move forward, they have been dependant on government support. Clare received some trades training and had some employment.

Two more children were born. Because of in-law and spousal control and abuse, Clare escaped to a far distant locale in Canada. The past haunts her. Emotional and increasing physical frailties have gradually ruled out attempts at employment.

Clare is passionately dedicated to her children and she is responsible in her parenting, conforming carefully to avoid the spectre of losing them. Social Workers have helped her in a number of ways, including short Sunday films in the home, which depict sound family practice. They have helped her set parameters. Feeling judged by society in Asia and in Canada, Clare has explored with me the matter of morals as seen in Canada. I have touched on the great diversity of attitudes and practices in our North American society. I have tried to explain God's best will for us as understood by Christians and how Christians too, can fall short. I found a lovely, illustrated book, which tells the story of Jesus in relation to the woman caught in adultery and threatened with stoning by judgmental men. "Let him who has not sinned cast the first stone." And they all left. (John 8:1-11)

Clare has considered her attitude toward the men friends who help out with the children's needs and with groceries. Sometimes she feels she must give something back. Despite past trauma, Clare is fond of men and attractive to them. In well-regulated moments, she seems deeply content when the right person is in her company. She dreams of a suitable, good marriage within which her bright children could prosper and she could enjoy her womanhood.

When I first was visiting with Clare, all was bad luck and doom though she could respond at times with remarkable maturity and warmth. One day she showed me an album of her drawings. When she was pregnant with her third child, she says her husband, controlling and abusive, talked endlessly into her ear.

In the third month of her pregnancy, she silently began to draw, practicing her circles and lines till she had them perfect. These drawing of Buddhas were her prayer for help. The response came when her baby was six months old. She was able to pack up her children, her album of drawings and the tools of the trade she had learned and to secretly move to a city far distant.

Clare has a well-kept shrine in a corner of her living area. She showed me one day her ritual when she lights candles around her personal Buddha figure and strikes a gong for the upward mobility of her ancestors.

My friend talks to her Buddha like a Christian might talk to Jesus, our brother and Lord. Does the great enlightenment hear her? Has she personalized Buddha as we in the Christian tradition personalize God?

The little frog on the island in one of the pictures was added by her eldest child, a son.

SURVIVAL STAMINA AND SPIRITUAL HOPE

Artist: Clare

SURVIVAL STAMINA AND SPIRITUAL HOPE

Artist: Clare

DUC — PHAT

THICH — CA . MAU . NI

DANG — THUYET . PHAP

SURVIVAL STAMINA AND SPIRITUAL HOPE

Artist: Clare

SURVIVAL STAMINA AND SPIRITUAL HOPE

Artist: Clare

SURVIVAL STAMINA AND SPIRITUAL HOPE

Artist: Clare

SURVIVAL STAMINA AND SPIRITUAL HOPE

Artist: Clare

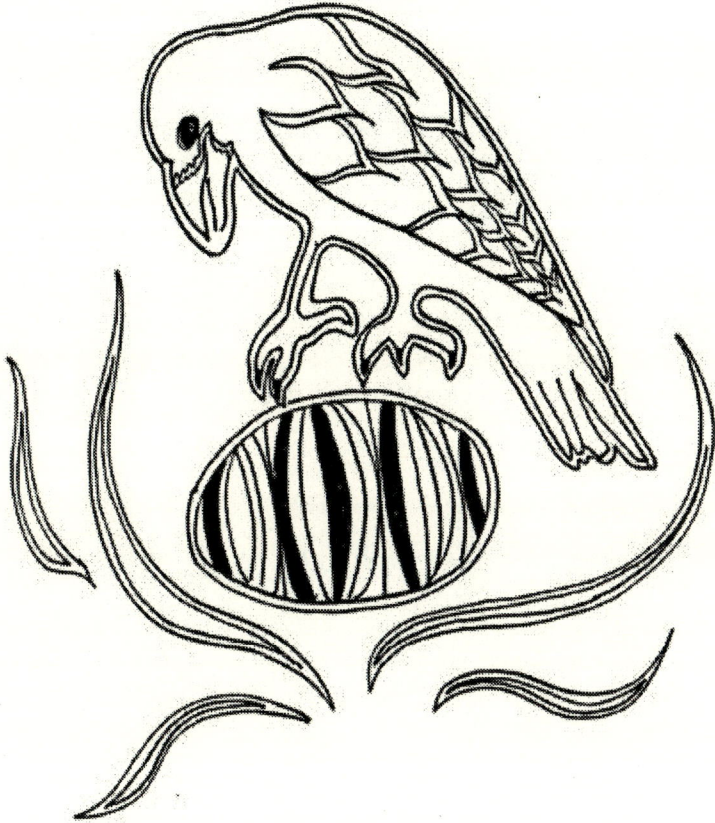

Belle Schiff

CONFESSION

In her travel book, copyright in 2003, "Somebody's Heart is Burning", Tanya Shaffer quotes a Ghanaian who is preparing her for a climb to a remote shrine as follows:

"The fetish is only a statue, but the spirit of a very strong ancestor, a chief, speaks to us through it, through the fetish priest."

I was interested to think who my fetish ancestors were and I will disclose my thoughts if you will bear with me during the following confession.

My paternal grandparents, of Lutheran and Roman Catholic heritages, living on another continent, I met only once and that was before my second birthday. Both warm and responsible adults, I have known them through photos and through story.

My maternal grandparents, both of Lutheran heritage, were not on our family scene either, but there were several visits throughout the years. My maternal grandfather had left his north German home forever and he had ventured to this new land alone. He was an example of a very responsible adult who became a good husband and caring father. He maintained several roles of leadership in his life vocation and among fellow immigrants. His stance in life clearly informs my perspectives. His wife, my grandmother, was an example of quiet faith and almost non-stop labor. At middle age she could still sing folksongs in a lilting voice, while doing her summer wash outdoors, to the delight of her younger children. In her old age, she was a gentle, sensible, spiritual presence.

A more ancient north German maternal ancestor, circa 1600 created a family crest which, in the 20th Century has overwhelmed some descendants with its injunction, "Ora et Labora", or "Pray and Work". It doesn't say "overwork", but by virtue of necessity, high goals, and firm conscience, that became the reality for some.

Belle Schiff

Hope, in its infinite guises, from the sublime to the heartrending to the mundane, from the realistic to the foolish, from the material to the emotional to the spiritual has expressed itself not only in centuries of forbears, but also in the many historical and contemporary humans of all cultures.

A high vision and limited strengths led me through some thorny paths. In times of desperation, I lived in shock. Sometimes I found an island of peace and love.

One day, when feeling and emotions had been in limbo for several years, when I was moving empty though the endless days, when even the flowers which grew so bravely and gloriously in the garden seemed stronger than I, then hope was perceived as only a tenacious silver lining to the grey which never led forward.

The day had come: time to end empty endurance, time for decisive action. I would prepare for the end by making that telephone call. It was a decisive moment as I walked down the summer street of bungalows, trees and flowers. In that split second a small drop of indescribable love seemingly from above and from behind, sparked my spirit into life.

CONFESSION

Artist: Coral Poser

Belle Schiff

Instantaneously, flowers and sky sprang into meaningful beauty. "What is this", I asked. "Whence does this come? It must be Jesus!"

Later that day, at the supper table, I experienced a warm, earthy cushion of love against my back. Again I asked, "Whence does this come? Before was Jesus", I thought, "and this is Martin Luther. He loves me too."

Today I think, "Perhaps I should add Bach and Beethoven and Brahms to my fetishes. They are warm priests of tender and celestial sound."

Sister Anna Ebert, Sister Martha Hansen, American deaconesses, and Christian martyr, Dietrich Bonhoeffer have been part of the world of my time.

Jesus was the Word by whom all things came to be: he is our very strong ancestor. All those I have mentioned and many more are his priests. By the waters of Baptism we enter God's eternal covenant.

Recently I bought a wall cross, made of a rock-like material with, at its centre, a four-part silver-painted square containing the word, GRACE. This symbol encapsulates the teaching of the Holy Spirit and my "fetish priests", reminding me of God the Father and God the Son's attitude toward my creature self, a glorious creature within His love.

2003

Scripture

1 Peter 1:3-5 Praise be to the God and Father of our Lord Jesus Christ! In his great mercy he has given us new birth into a living hope through the resurrection of Jesus Christ from the dead, and into an inheritance that can never perish, spoil or fade—kept in heaven for you, who through faith are shielded by God's power until the coming of the salvation that is ready to be revealed in the last time.

1 John 3:1 How great is the love the Father has lavished on us, that we should be called children of God! And that is what we are!

2b But we know that when he appears, we shall be like him, for we shall see him as he is. 3. Everyone who has this hope in him purifies himself, just as he is pure.

Revelation 22:20b Amen, Come, Lord Jesus.

Photographer: Belle Schiff

"Thank you, dear Reader"

About the Author

Born in 1930, Belle Schiff had a country childhood in Western Canada, in the parkland area of Alberta. She was nurtured in the Christian faith by God-fearing parents. During her early school years she intervened when negative manipulation by schoolmates threatened the wellbeing of some. Her life's journey has taken her from rural settings, to towns and cities in four Canadian provinces and four American states. In the eastern U.S. she did postgraduate studies in social work. Since then she has gained insights within the Green Party of Canada and at the International Bioregional Gatherings. Travel has taken her to Germany, Holland, Switzerland, Jordan, Israel and Mozambique. In 1999 she helped found the Kapasseni Project Committee which assists a once-demolished Mozambican village in its recovery and ongoing development.

Printed in the United States
23470LVS00006B/121-255

9 781418 420727